D0376009

JURASSIC SURVIVAL GUIDE

DANGER!
KEEP OUT: LIVE DINOSAUR AREA

NOTES FROM THE FIELD

Scientists don't really know how this happened, but I do. I was asked to join a Japanese expedition to a remote island in the South Pacific. I was briefed along the way. Here are my notes from that voyage:

Japanese scientists have found frozen dinosaurs intact on Antarctica. As the ice continues to melt, the beasts are being uncovered.

They brought the beasts back to the lab for analysis and were able to extract DNA samples from several different dinosaurs, including the dreaded meat-eaters.

For fear of public panic, they put these dinosaurs on a remote island in the South Pacific where they could keep an eye on them.

Fortunately, and unfortunately, the dinosaurs not only survived, but thrived.

IT'S ALL MY FAULT!

THEY DID HATCH INTO BABY DINOSAURS!

November 11, 2011

I brought back a few eggs as a souvenir. "What was the harm." They probably wouldn't hatch, or so I thought.

I didn't know what to do. I panicked and released them into the Everglades, hoping that one of our top predators would take care of my mistake. As with all invasive species, they not only survived but are thriving in the warm environment. There is plenty of food and warm weather. It's the perfect storm. Last year, they started spreading out to claim more territory. That's why I wrote this survival guide. It's your only chance.

You'll need to be ready when they get to your neighborhood. This guide will give you the information you need to survive. Learn from it, or the human species will become extinct.

LIFE IN THE JURASSIC WORLD

At the start of the Early Jurassic Period (197 million years ago), the giant supercontinent Pangaea broke up, forming the beginning of the world that we know today. There were huge volcanic eruptions with rivers of lava and clouds of poisonous gases. The earth shook with high-magnitude earthquakes as this supercontinent separated into smaller ones.

Land that had been part of the interior of the huge continent was now the coastline of smaller continents, and the climate began to change as well.

PANGAEA

Eurasia

North
America

South
America

Africa

Antarctica

Australia

WHAT WE THOUGHT

People have been wondering about dinosaurs forever: what they were and what they looked like. People in all cultures have found dinosaur bones. They know that these were once living animals, but not much else.

Fossils are the remains of long-dead plants and animals that have been buried by sand or mud soon after death. The harder parts, like teeth and bones, may be preserved.

What we know keeps changing. And it will change even more when the Dinosaur Invasion begins.

THINGS WE KNOW:

1. Dinosaurs died out approximately 66 million years ago.

2. Fossilized dinosaur bones, skin, eggs, feathers, poop, and footprints have been found all over the world.

3. Some dinosaurs had feathers.

4. The Mesozoic Era lasted for 165 million years. It is broken into three periods: the Triassic, the Jurassic, and the Cretaceous Periods.

5. Some, but not all, paleontologists believe that dinosaurs were **warm-blooded** animals.

6. New dinosaur fossils are being found every day (like the ones found by the Japanese scientists).

KNOW YOUR ENEMIES

There are a lot of myths and legends about monsters and dragons that came about because of dinosaur fossils. Are these half-truths? Is your imagination playing tricks on you or have the dinosaurs been hiding in plain sight? If you're going to survive the dinosaur invasion, you'll need to know the facts.

Knights slaying a Carnotaurus?

Perhaps St. George slew a dinosaur instead.

Plane over Los Angeles or soaring dinosaur?

Loch Ness monster – Cryptid or surviving Apatosaurus?

o find out more about dinosaurs, look on pages 40—41.

EAT OR BE EATEN!

WILL THEY EAT ME?

Let's get down to what you really want to know. Can I catch and eat a dinosaur, or am I going to be some T-rex's next meal? The short answer is "Yes" and "Yes."

It's really pretty simple . . . and boring. Plant-eaters walked around slowly, eating and going to the bathroom. A majority of dinosaurs were plant-eaters.

The meat-eaters lived more exciting lives by hunting for prey, but then, like modern lions, they probably had to sleep as much as twenty hours a day. And they may have missed their prey nine out of ten times.

Would you eat a Brachiosaurus steak? A normal-size Brachiosaurus could potentially feed a small town for months.

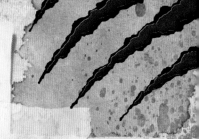

Dinosaurs weren't instinctively violent, even the meat eaters. It is more likely that they fought for territory, food, or nest protection, like modern-day animals.

Some dinosaurs lived in herds, like deer. Apatosaurus is a good example. Other dinosaurs lived alone, like bears. T-rex has been seen alone most of the time. But there have been times when two or more of them have hunted in the same area.

There is evidence that some dinosaurs were able to walk, run, and dig, but they weren't very good at climbing. Watch out for Sinornithosaurus. It was seen in the trees. How it got there, we aren't sure.

Have observed the dinosaurs on the island with large crests, horns, or frills. They are prancing around like peacocks trying to attract mates. One little dinosaur put up his feathered frill when I got too close. Cool defensive move, but the bite hurt!

Dinosaurs, whether plant-eaters or meat-eaters needed their senses to find food, but they also needed them to survive attacks and the harsh environment.

SMELL

They'll smell you before you smell them. In some plant-eaters and meat-eaters, the part of the brain that is responsible for smell was big. Scientists believe that this shows that the dinosaurs' sense of smell was very important in finding plants or prey, detecting predators, or maybe finding a mate.

SIGHT

Dinosaurs will outdo you in the sight department, too. Most plant-eating dinosaurs had eyes on the sides of their heads, so they could see their surroundings, like a horse. However, meat-eaters had relatively big, forward-facing eyes, like humans do, that were used to judge distances to prey.

HEARING

Dinosaurs can out-hear you, too. They'll hear you coming, and they'll be able to track you this way

On the island, we have observed the plant-eaters listening for predators or the warning calls of other dinosaurs, just like birds do. On the other hand, the meat-eaters listen carefully for sounds of their prey.

Frequency means the number of sound waves that pass a fixed point each second.

Low frequency = less sound waves

High frequency = more sound waves

KILLED!

Dinosaurs had big bellies. Plant-eaters could devour vast quantities of plants in a single feeding. Meat-eaters were excellent hunters, gobbling down their prey in one big gulp.

Scientists believe that some of the meat-eating dinosaurs hunted like modern-day cats by stalking and ambushing their prey. Sinocalliopteryx (say it like this: SIGH-no-CAL-ee-OP-ter-icks) was found with flying prey in its belly. We saw this little dinosaur stalking birds on the island.

Other scientists have found evidence that some dinosaurs hunted in packs, like wolves and lions do today. Six months into our stay on the island, we witnessed a pack of Deinonychus (pronounced die-NON-ih-cuss) hunting a Camptosaurus herd. The Deinonychus pack was ruthless in the pursuit of their prey. We watched in amazement as the five-member pack devoured most of the carcass. They hid the rest of the kill under a pile of leaves for a late-night snack.

COULD YOU OUTRUN, OUTSMART, OR OUTLAST A DINOSAUR?

As long as you're smarter than an ostrich, you'd outsmart a dinosaur. Outrun? You won't be able to outrun a meat-eater. Tyrannosaurus Rex could run approximately 10 to 25 mph (16 to 40 kph), but some of the smaller dinosaurs could move faster than that. The average human can run approximately 6 mph (9.7 kph). Can you outlast a dinosaur? If you can run for a long distance, like several miles (kilometers), you might be able to outlast a dinosaur. But remember, they can be tricky when they're hunting.

TOP TEN MOST DEADLY DINOSAURS

There were a lot of scary things happening on the island: giant mosquitoes, dragonflies, flying reptiles, volcanic eruptions, and of course, dinosaurs! Here are a few of the most deadly dinosaurs that we saw. Take notes, they might be coming to your neighborhood next.

ANKYLOSAURUS

Ankylosaurus is often compared to a tank or bus. That club tail, indestructible armor, and ability to survive and adapt to the changing environment all make this heavy-duty dinosaur one you'll need to watch out for. This dinosaur lived in the Late Cretaceous Period, about 65 to 75 million years ago, in what is now the western U.S. and Canada. Paleontologists believe this plant-eating dino was one of the last to face extinction.

Pronunciation:
ank-ILL-oh-SORE-us
Name meaning:
Fused Lizard
Size: 35 ft. (11 m) long
6 ft. (2 m) wide
4 ft. (1.5 m) tall
Weight: 6 tons (5.5 tonnes)
Plant-eater

SINORNITHOSAURUS

Sinornithosaurus was a feathered dinosaur with giant teeth. It lived in the Early Cretaceous Period. It is in the same family as Velociraptor. They are small, quick, and agile hunters. Some scientists think that Sinornithosaurus is venomous, but that hasn't been proven. If it is true, it would make this little dinosaur more deadly than it looks.

SINORNITHOSAURUS SKULL

Pronunciation:
sign-OR-nith-oh-SORE-us
Name meaning:
Chinese Bird-Lizard
Size: 3 ft. (1 m) long
18 in. (46 cm) tall
Weight: 20 lbs. (9 kg)
Speed: 25 mph (40 kph)
Meat-eater

TROODON

It isn't this dinosaur's size or sharp teeth that puts it on the most deadly list. Troodon weighed about the same as an adult human, and its teeth were sharp, but not scary looking. What set this dino apart was its incredibly big brain compared to other meat-eaters. It is thought that Troodon hunted at night because of its large eyes. A pack of Troodon could easily hunt you in the dark. You'll have to be able to see in the dark to survive this deadly dino.

This small, feathered dinosaur had long, slender hind legs and grasping hands with two large retractable claws on the second toe of each foot. Fossils have been found far into the Arctic Circle.

RAZOR-SHARP TEETH!

Pronunciation:
TRUE-oh-don
Name meaning:
Wounding Tooth
Size: 6 ft. (2 m) long
Weight: 150 lbs. (68 kg)
Speed: 24 mph (39 kph)
Omnivore (ate both plants and meat)

ALLOSAURUS

Allosaurus was a huge meat-eating dinosaur that lived during the Late Jurassic Period. This big dinosaur had knife-like teeth that were up to 4 in. (10 cm) long.

WARNING!

This dinosaur is as tall as you and two of your friends standing on each other's shoulders. Its teeth are as big as your whole hand, and it runs faster than you. Stay out of this dinosaur's way, or you'll end up a nice, little snack.

Pronunciation:
al-oh-SORE-us
Name meaning:
Different Lizard
Size: 16.4 ft. (5 m) tall;
39.5 ft. (12 m) long
Weight: 1.5 tons (1.4 t)
Speed: 21 mph (39 kph)
Meat-eater

CARNOTAURUS

We watched the Carnotaurus on the island take down a large Apatosaurus and eat it in large gulps. They run fas and have an excellent sense of smell. A Carnotaurus in your neighborhood will be like a bull with sharp teeth in a china shop.

This huge meat-eating dinosaur had a big head, bull-like horns, tiny, sharp teeth, and itty-bitty arms (only 1.5 ft. (50 cm) long). Carnotaurus lived during the Late Cretaceous Period.

TOO CLOSE!!!

Pronunciation:
 CAR-no-TORE-us
Name meaning:
 Meat-eating Bull
Size: 13 ft. (4 m) tall;
 30 ft. (9 m) long
Weight: 2.25 tons (2 T)
Speed: 25 mph (40 kph)
Meat-eater

VELOCIRAPTOR

Velociraptor is not a pet. It is a sneaky, dangerous predator with sharp teeth. And in your neighborhood, they would hunt you like a pack of hungry wolves.

This small, feathered dinosaur lived during the Late Cretaceous Period. It had two sickle-shaped claws on each foot. Some experts believe Velociraptor hunted in packs. There is new evidence that shows that Velociraptor used its 2.5 in. (6.5 cm) claws to climb and grip prey.

Velociraptor claw found on the island

Pronunciation:
vel-OSS-ih-rap-tor
Name meaning:
Speedy Thief
Size: 2.5 ft. (76 cm) tall;
5.9 ft. (2 m) long
Weight: 40 lbs. (18 kg)
Speed: 24 mph (39 kph)
Meat-eater

29

UTAHRAPTOR

Velociraptor and Deinonychus are usually the stars of the show, but Utahraptor was a killing machine. It was bigger, stronger, and faster than the other two dinosaurs. Its huge 12 in. (30.5 cm) claws were used for ripping and slashing at prey. It is thought to have hunted like a cat, inflicting deep puncture wounds and gashes during its ambush. Then it sat back and waited for its prey to bleed to death.

Pronunciation:
YOU-tah-RAP-tor
Name meaning:
Utah thief
Size: 23 ft. (7 m) long, head to tail
Weight: 1,500 lbs. (680 kg)
Speed: 20 mph (32 kph)
Meat-eater

SPINOSAURUS

Even though this dinosaur mostly eats fish, on the island we saw it attack a T-rex...and win! This is not a dinosaur to mess with.

Spinosaurus looked like a very large crocodile that walked on two feet and had a huge sail on its back. It was probably the largest meat-eater that ever walked on Earth. This big dino ate fish that it trapped in its cage-like front teeth. Spinosaurus lived during the Middle Cretaceous Period (95 million years ago).

Pronunciation:
  SPINE-o-SORE-us
Name meaning:
  Spine Lizard
Size: 23 ft. (7 m) tall;
  56 ft. (17 m) long
Weight: 22 tons (20 T)
Speed: 25 mph (40 kph)
Fish-eater

A complete skeleton of Spinosaurus has not been found, so its size is just an educated guess.

GIGANOTOSAURUS

Giganotosaurus was one of the largest meat-eating dinosaurs, even larger than T. rex. It lived in the Late Cretaceous Period in what is now South America. Its thin, pointed tail would have helped it with quick turns. Along with its agility, it had 8 in. (20.5 cm) dagger-like teeth. Its entire body was made for gripping, ripping, and tearing into prey ... like you!

Pronunciation: Gee-gah-NOTE-oh-SORE-us
Name meaning: Giant Southern Lizard
Size: 23 ft. (7 m) tall, 43 ft. (13 m) long
Weight: 8 tons (7.25 t)
Speed: 31 mph (51 kph)
Meat-eater

TYRANNOSAURUS REX

T. rex, as it's better known, was a big, bad dinosaur. It could eat up to 500 lbs. (230 kg) of meat and bones in one bite. One T. rex fossil was found with teeth that were 13 in. (33 cm) long. T. rex lived during the Late Cretaceous Period in what is now western North America. T. rex could sniff out prey as well as any great white shark and had the vision of a hawk. It possibly had the most powerful bite of any animal on Earth, ever! Don't get caught by this monster!

Pronunciation:
Tih-RAN-oh-SORE-us Reks

Name meaning:
Tyrant Lizard King

Size: 13 ft. (4 m) tall, 43 ft. (13 m) long

Weight: 8 tons (7 T)

Speed: 25 mph (40 kph)

Meat-eater

INVASIVE SPECIES AROUND THE WORLD

Invasive species are bad news. They are animals that don't belong in an area. It can destroy the local environment and even endanger humans. Here are a few invasive species that are wreaking havoc, maybe even in your neighborhood. Let's hope that the dinosaurs that were released don't become more invasive species.

Cane toads produce a poison that is deadly to many species, and they are difficult to kill. These toads have been spotted coming out of brush fires and hopping away after being run over by a car.

The Asian tiger mosquito is a black-and-white–marked mosquito and it kills millions of people every year. It is a carrier of the West Nile virus and dengue fever, among other diseases.

The snakehead fish is a native of Asia with sharp, sharklike teeth and an appetite for blood. They can reach lengths of more than 3 ft. (1 m), and lay up to 75,000 eggs per year. The snakehead fish can breathe through primitive lungs and can migrate on land for up to four days.

Black rats carried the plague throughout Europe.

Burmese pythons have escaped or were released into the wild. They can reach lengths up to 22 ft. (6.5 m). One even tried to eat an alligator.

DINOSAUR INVASION!

It is just a matter of time before these monstrous animals become the next invasive species. Your neighborhood is ground zero for the invasion!

KNOW YOUR DINOSAUR FACTS:

We don't know exactly how long dinosaurs lived. However, they'll live long enough to cause trouble in the environment and in your neighborhood.

Dinosaurs lived everywhere on Earth. The new dinos have adapted well to today's climate.

Some dinosaurs had brains the size of peas. But that doesn't mean that they couldn't outsmart you if they're hungry.

Dinosaurs dominated the earth for almost 150 million years. They can do it again.

Dinosaurs are considered warm-blooded by many paleontologists. This means they will be able to survive the cold winters.

Some dinosaurs had more than 1,000 teeth. And some dinos could replace their teeth as needed.

Let's look at some dinosaurs you might encounter when the invasion begins. You'll want to know how to survive their attacks.

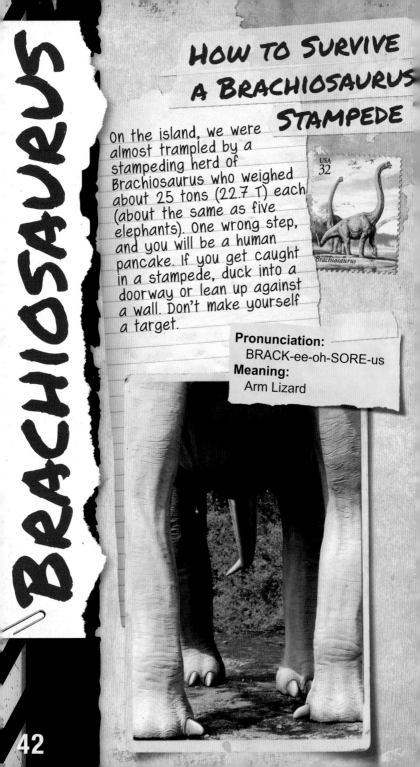

HOW TO SURVIVE A BRACHIOSAURUS STAMPEDE

On the island, we were almost trampled by a stampeding herd of Brachiosaurus who weighed about 25 tons (22.7 T) each (about the same as five elephants). One wrong step, and you will be a human pancake. If you get caught in a stampede, duck into a doorway or lean up against a wall. Don't make yourself a target.

USA
32

Brachiosaurus

Pronunciation:
BRACK-ee-oh-SORE-us
Meaning:
Arm Lizard

Brachiosaurus lived during the Jurassic Period. It was among the tallest dinosaurs at 40 to 50 ft. (12 to 16 m) tall and 85 ft. (26 m) long. It had a thick jawbone with 52 spoon-shaped teeth that were perfect for stripping vegetation. It is likely that Brachiosaurus ate up to 400 lbs. (181 kg) of leafy greens every day. They may be stripping the trees in the park soon!

How to Survive a Triceratops Charge

Triceratops is like a giant rhinoceros that can move at 16 mph (26 kph). When a Triceratops charges, it is more than likely trying to scare you, but do you want to take that chance? Based on those horns and its sheer size, Triceratops is not a dinosaur to mess with. If you are faced with a charging Triceratops, get out of the way. A safe place would be with a lot of people or on a large vehicle, like a bus.

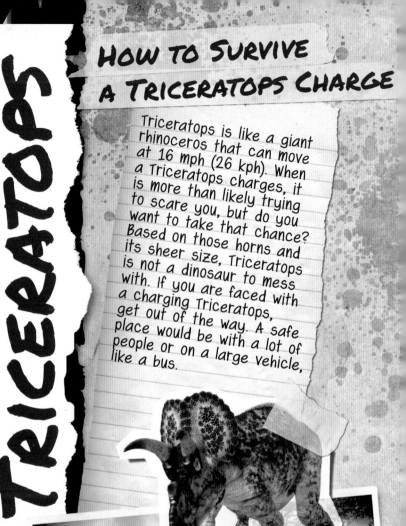

Triceratops had three horns on its head and a large bony frill behind its head. Its body shape was similar to a rhinoceros, at 10 ft. (3 m) tall and 30 ft. (9 m) long, and it weighed 6.75 tons (6 T). Triceratops lived during the Late Cretaceous Period in the forested areas of what is now Western North America. Its mouth was full of teeth that formed a continuous surface and acted like giant scissors. They were perfect for cutting vegetation.

HOW TO SURVIVE A DEFENSIVE PSITTACOSAURUS

We found evidence that Psittacosaurus defended its young. It used its beak to bite off one of our assistant's fingers after he got too close to the babies. If you want to keep all of your limbs, stay clear of this guy. It's not difficult to do since they move so slow.

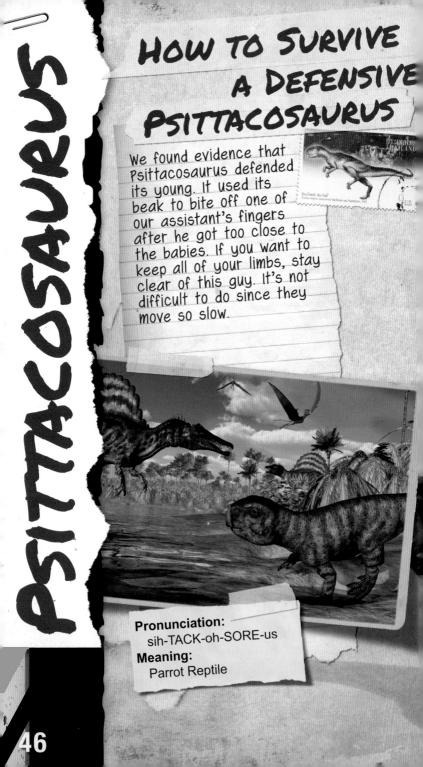

Pronunciation:
sih-TACK-oh-SORE-us
Meaning:
Parrot Reptile

Psittacosaurus had a short, curved beak and small horns on its cheeks. This dinosaur lived during the Cretaceous Period. It was about 5 ft. (1.5 m) long, 2 ft. (60 cm) tall, and weighed about 100 lbs. (45 kg).

How to Survive a Camptosaurus Stampede

On the island, we watched a Camptosaurus herd stampede because it was being chased by a pair of Allosaurus. Not only do you have to watch out for the meat-eaters in this situation, but the Camptosaurus almost ran us over like a herd of horses. Just step out of the way, but watch for whatever is chasing the herd.

Pronunciation:
CAMP-toe-SORE-us
Meaning:
Bent Lizard

Camptosaurus USA 32

Camptosaurus was a plant-eating dinosaur that spent a lot of its time on its hind legs, but it probably moved around on all fours. It had a horse-like snout with a beak for snipping vegetation. It had hundreds of grinding teeth in the back of its mouth and cheeks, a lot like a human's. This means it could hold food in its mouth as it chewed.

Pacific island. A pair of Allosaurus sneaking up on a herd of Camptosaurus.

MICRORAPTOR

A Microraptor attack will come from the trees. The predator will drop down like a hawk or eagle after its prey ... you! Seek shelter immediately. The safest place is in a building with the windows and doors closed.

Microraptor was a small dinosaur with long feathers designed for gliding. Each foot had claws that were perfect for catching prey and climbing. It probably lived in the trees, gliding from branch to branch in search of prey. This meat-eating dinosaur lived in the Cretaceous Period and was about 2 ft. (60 cm) long, 5 ft. (1.5 m) tall, and weighed about 4 lbs. (2 kg). It ate fish and small animals.

Pronunciation:
MY-crow-rap-tore
Meaning:
Small Thief

EORAPTOR

HOW TO SURVIVE AN EORAPTOR ATTACK

Eoraptor, which isn't a raptor at all, eats small animals and **scavenges** as well. This little dino is one to watch out for. It's quick and agile. And let's hope it doesn't hunt in packs. Your best bet for survival is to remain silent and let it move on. If it starts hissing, you're in trouble. RUN!

Eoraptor is one of the oldest-known dinosaurs, and lived during the Triassic Period, 250 to 200 million years ago. They were about 3 ft. (1 m) long and weighed about 20 lbs. (9 kg). It walked on two legs, had a long tail, five-fingered hands, and a mouth filled with sharp teeth.

Pronunciation:
EE-oh-rap-tore
Meaning:
Dawn Thief

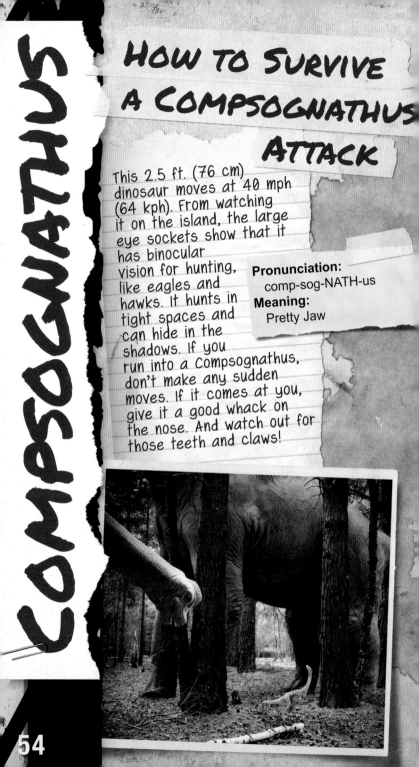

How to Survive a Compsognathus Attack

This 2.5 ft. (76 cm) dinosaur moves at 40 mph (64 kph). From watching it on the island, the large eye sockets show that it has binocular vision for hunting, like eagles and hawks. It hunts in tight spaces and can hide in the shadows. If you run into a Compsognathus, don't make any sudden moves. If it comes at you, give it a good whack on the nose. And watch out for those teeth and claws!

Pronunciation: comp-sog-NATH-us
Meaning: Pretty Jaw

54

This small, birdlike dinosaur had a skinny body and a long snout with a mouth full of small, sharp teeth. Compsognathus lived during the Jurassic Period, and it hunted lizards and other small prey.

HOW TO SURVIVE A DIPLODOCUS TAIL WHIP

DIPLODOCUS

One morning, we heard the loud crack of a bullwhip. One of our photographers was hit in the back by the tail of a Diplodocus. This dino may be slow, but that tail is fast and can leave huge gashes in your skin. Seek medical attention as soon as possible.

Diplodocus on the island.

Pronunciation:
dip-LOW-doe-kuss
Meaning:
Double Beam

This massive plant-eater had a superlong neck and tail. Diplodocus lived during the Jurassic Period in what is now western North America. It had about 40 teeth, all of which pointed forward and were used for stripping vegetation. Diplodocus's poop was a huge amount of liquid dropped from about 10 ft. (3 m) high. Make sure you are never under the backside of a Diplodocus, or bring a heavy-duty umbrella!

Tanzania 35/.
DIPLODOCUS

Look what we found in the Everglades. The invasion may have already started.

HOW TO SURVIVE A GARGOYLEOSAURUS GAS ATTACK

It is unlikely that this docile dino would attack, but if it gets scared, watch out for that clubbed tail! Oh, and hold your nose! All of the foliage that it eats creates a lot of gas. It's bound to be pretty smelly around this big guy. Those farts are deadly.

Gargoyleosaurus was an armor-plated ancestor of Ankylosaurus. This plant-eater was low to the ground and moved very slowly. Moving at a snail's pace and eating foliage that was close to the ground made for an unfortunate thing about Gargoyleosaurus. With a belly full of foliage, it farted . . . a lot.

Pronunciation:
GAR-goil-oh-SORE-us
Meaning:
Gargoyle Lizard

HOW TO SURVIVE A FRIGHTENED STEGOSAURUS

With its poor eyesight and lack of intelligence, Stegosaurus had to develop other means of protection. The 17 bony plates on its back were huge, with the largest plate measuring 24 in. (60 cm) tall and wide. It also had a spiked tail for added protection. Since this big guy couldn't move very fast (about 4 mph or 6 kph), you could easily get out of its way. However, that spiked tail could take you out. Watch for the windup!

Pronunciation:
STEG-oh-SORE-us
Meaning:
Roof Lizard

Stegosaurus ate plants and fruits using its small, triangular, flat teeth. This gentle giant stood about 12 ft. (3.5 m) tall, was about 30 ft. (9 m) long, and weighed almost 4 tons (3 T). Stegosaurus had a small brain and poor eyesight, so these dinos may have lived in herds for protection.

HOW TO SURVIVE A QIANZHOUSAURUS ASSAULT

This 30 ft. (9 m) tall meat-eater isn't a top predator, but it's still dangerous! We watched several of them hunt down a full-grown Triceratops, which isn't good news for you. Your best bet for survival is an alarm system alerting you to when a Qianzhousaurus pack is hunting you.

Pronunciation:
SHEE-ahn-zhoo-SORE-us
Meaning:
Qianzhou Lizard

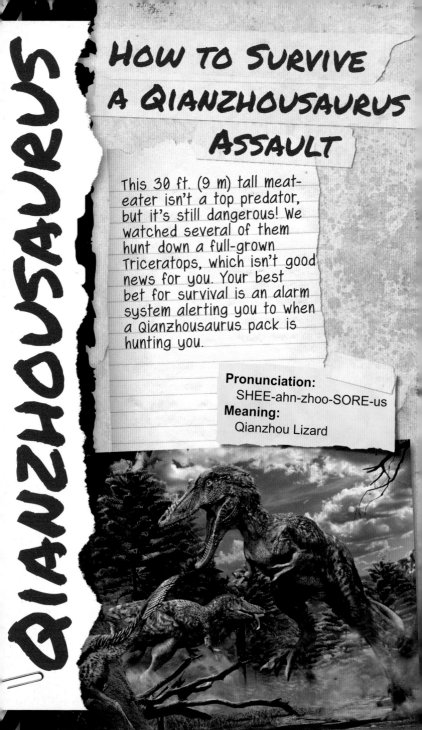

A newly discovered dinosaur, Qianzhousaurus lived in what is now southern China about the time when the dinosaurs became extinct. This T. rex cousin was a birdlike dino that was a fearsome hunter. Its nickname is "Pinocchio rex," because of its long snout, covered with a small row of horns. Scientists believe that these lean, mean dinosaurs lived all over Asia.

IF YOU'RE GOING TO SURVIVE . . .

. . . you'll need to know these important survival skills:

How to find food.

How to get water and purify it.

How to repair clothing.

The basics of cleanliness, like brushing your teeth.

Basic first aid.

How to start a fire.

How to defend yourself by being smart.

Training your mind to expect the unexpected.

Understanding that the world is not the way it used to be.

Items most useful for your survival.

STAY AWAY

YOUR JURASSIC SURVIVAL KIT

LARGE
BACKPACK

Most important bit of gear is the backpack that carries it all! Make sure it's sturdy and weatherproof.

CLOTHES

Pack your quick-dry pants, t-shirt, hoodie or hat, raincoat, leather belt, hiking boots, socks, and glasses.

TOILET PAPER
AND QUICK-DRY TOWEL

Yeah, you're going to need both of these. Make sure you stash extra toilet paper, just in case.

DUCT TAPE

Always good in a bind.

CRANK-POWERED FLASHLIGHT

No batteries—it's powered by you!

FIRST AID KIT
AND ANTIBACTERIAL SOAP/SPRAY

Medications, pain relievers, wet wipes, sunblock, lip balm, and your antibacterial soap or spray.

ESSENTIAL EDIBLES

Protein bars, trail mix, and hard candy provide a quick fix when you're on the run. Make sure to pack a ready-to-eat meal (MRE) when you need something more filling.

1-LITER METAL WATER BOTTLE

Keep it full of fresh water at all times.

GENERAL SUPPLIES

Binoculars, scissors, signal mirror, paracord, string, and a few fishing hooks should be in your kit on all terrain.

CAMP TOOLS

Whether you're purifying water or starting a fire, make sure to carry a magnifying glass, shovel, and bandana. See pages 74, 75, and 77 for more info!

ENTERTAINMENT

A deck of cards, or other small games, can keep boredom away.

Learning basic first aid is a good idea for any situation, but it becomes very important when you're trying to survive.

Ask your parents to help you find a basic First Aid course near you . . . **before it's too late!**

FINDING FOOD

HUNT LIKE A DINOSAUR

Whether you're a meat-eater, plant-eater, or a bit of both, you'll need to find food within a few days. You might be able to find food that you always ate for little while, but what do you do after that?

A PLANT-EATING DINOSAUR HUNTS FOR FOOD BY FORAGING.

You can also forage for berries and other wild plants to help you survive the dinosaur invasion. However, there are a lot of poisonous plants out there, so it would be a really good idea to learn from an expert what wild plants are okay to eat in your area.

A MEAT-EATING DINOSAUR USES ITS SENSE OF SMELL TO HUNT FOR PREY.

This might be difficult for you, since a human's sense of smell is not nearly as good as a theropod's. For example, you might be able to smell a little bit of sugar in a cup of water, but a meat-eating dinosaur can smell that same little bit in a million gallons (3.8 million L) of water.

Try an experiment:

Blindfold a friend and have him or her sniff different types of food. See how many he or she can guess correctly.

LET'S GO FISHING

Don't have a rod to fish for your meal?

Fishing line:
Using a bit of thread, dental floss, pieces of wire, or twisted bark, you can fashion a fishing line pretty easily.

Lures:
Some pieces of cloth, bits of feathers, or bright metal earrings make great fishing lures.

Make a bait fish funnel trap:

Ask a parent to help you cut a 2-liter plastic bottle using scissors. Cut about 1/3 of the way down from the bottle mouth.

1. Place several stones in the bottom of the bottle to weigh it down.

2. Put your bait in the bottom part of the bottle. A little bit of bread or worms is fine.

3. Turn the top half upside down within the bottle bottom, so the mouth is facing down.

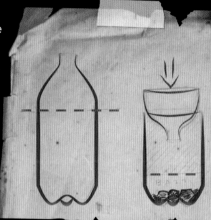

4. Submerge your funnel trap and wait for your fish.

Note: To catch bigger fish, use the line and lures. Use your funnel trap to catch little fish to use as bait for bigger catches.

WARNING:

Once you've found a good fishing spot, keep a sharp eye out! You're not the only one looking for a tasty catch.

Spinosaurus doing a little fishing of its own.

COOKING AND STORING FOOD

If you're hiding from dinosaurs all the time, you're going to want a warm meal now and then. Always cook and eat your food quickly. Remember, dinosaurs can smell your food from long distances, and they'll be looking for a quick, easy meal, too.

MAKING A FIRE

All good fires start with tinder. Look for dried moss, dead leaves, or dried bark. Tinder catches fire easily.

Warning!
If you are not in an emergency situation, have an adult help you build a fire.

KINDLING

Kindling gets the fire going. Look for thin dried twigs.

FUEL

The fuel keeps the fire burning. Dried sticks at least a thumb's width work great.

1. Choose a good spot away from grasses, bushes, and low-hanging tree branches.

2. Make a platform on bare ground.

3. Place a bunch of tinder in the platform area.

4. Put kindling on top of the tinder.

5. Place the fuel around the kindling in a tepee shape.

6. Light the tinder with a magnifying glass.

COOKING OVER A FIRE

Cooking over a fire has the advantages of cooking your food, keeping you warm, and protecting you from wild animals, including dinosaurs. Cook your food quickly using a green stick with a sharp point at the end. Push a small piece of meat onto the stick and put it over the fire. Make sure you cook your meat all the way through. NEVER eat raw or uncooked meats. You're not a dinosaur!

75

FINDING WATER

Water is a top priority! Humans will only survive about three days without fresh water. Happily, there are a lot of places where you can find water. But it will need to be purified before you can drink it. You'll also have to be aware of dinosaurs, because they need even more water than you do.

WHERE TO FIND WATER

Streams

Rain

Plants (some carry water in their leaves and roots)

Collect dew

If you aren't in an emergency situation, ask an adult to help you.

WATCH OUT for wild animals and the dinosaurs—they'll be looking for water, too.

PURIFYING WATER

Water found in the wild contains bacteria that can make you sick. That is not what you want when you're trying to fight off dinosaurs. Always purify any water that you drink or cook with.

1. Filter your water by pouring it through a clean sock or nylon stocking lined with a bandanna or a handful of sand.

2. Boil the filtered water for five minutes.

3. When it is cool, store the water in a clean container and keep it in the shade.

Never wait until you run out of water to get more.

COLLECTING WATER

There are several different ways you can collect water. Here are a few to get you started.

METHOD 1: RAINWATER AND DEW COLLECTION

1. Stretch out a waterproof sheet or tarp.

2. Stake it to the ground with twigs.

3. Place a large container at one edge of the tarp and place small stones toward that edge that will lead into the container.

4. Catch rainwater and dew in the container.

Note: The moisture from the ground will get heated by the sun and begin to evaporate. Condensation will form on the underside of the plastic sheet and run down into your container. Filter the water and store it in a clean container in the shade.

Method 2:

Belowground Catchment

1. Gather a plastic sheet, a shovel or trowel, a large tin can, and a small rock.

2. Choose an area that gets a lot of sunlight for most of the day.

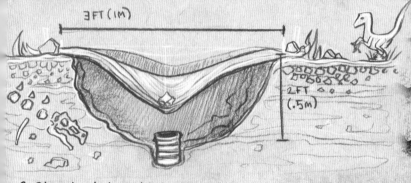

3. Dig a bowl-shaped hole about 3 ft. (1 m) across and 2 ft. (60 cm) deep. Add a slightly deeper center section to hold your container.

4. Place the tin can in the center of the hole.

5. Place the plastic sheet over the hole and let it hang down about 18 in. (45.5 cm), directly over the container. This will look like an inverted cone.

6. Add soil or rocks around the edge of the hole to hold the plastic sheet in place.

7. Place your small rock in the center of the sheet.

79

STAY HEALTHY

Eating well and having fresh, filtered water is extremely important for your health, but so is staying clean. It will help you avoid diseases in a survival situation or anytime. Here are a few things you must do:

1. Wash your hands after handling anything and especially after going to the bathroom. Bacteria can get on your food and make you sick.

2. Keep your clothes clean, or you might wind up with a skin disease, infection, or parasites.

3. Brushing your teeth is always important, but especially in a survival situation. Getting a mouth infection or large cavity can be life threatening without dental care. If a toothbrush, toothpaste, and floss are not available, keep your mouth and teeth clean by using a small stick wrapped with a clean cloth with salt on it. Rub it across your teeth and gums.

4. Keep your feet clean because they may be your only means of transportation. It's best to keep them dry, and clip those toenails. Check your feet daily for blisters or sores. A massage will also help relax the muscles and joints of the foot, especially if you've been walking a long way.

5. Get enough sleep! Resting your body will give you the energy to keep going in a survival situation and allow you to think and respond clearly to any event.

AVOIDING ILLNESS:
QUICK GUIDE

» **Purify your water** (see page 77)

» **Create a latrine** at least 200 yds. (183 m) away from your base camp to avoid contaminating your resources.

» **Wash your hands** before handling food or drinking water, and after handling anything else.

» Make it a habit to **clean your teeth and mouth** twice a day.

» If possible, wear clothing to protect yourself from insect bites. And keep your clothing clean.

» **Keep your clothes dry,** so your body temperature won't drop.

» Always get at least seven to eight hours of rest each day.

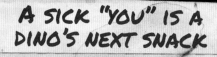

A SICK "YOU" IS A DINO'S NEXT SNACK

WHERE WOULD THE DINOSAURS BE HIDING, HUNTING, OR GETTING WATER?

AND MOST IMPORTANT, WHERE WILL YOU BE?

How to Deal with a Dinosaur

The Mental Game

If the dinosaur invasion has begun, you'll need to know how to deal with dinosaurs, which are looking for water and a meal. It will be very important for you to be on your A game.

You're way smarter than any dinosaur, but they are cunning and use all of their senses to hunt. Your emotions of fear, sadness, loneliness, and anxiety are there to keep you alive. Use them. Practice them now, so when you're in a survival situation you'll be prepared. Here are some things you can do to prepare your mind for survival:

» **Adapt to any situation.** Use ingenuity to figure out a solution. Whining and complaining about the situation will not change it. Remember, there is always more than one solution to any problem.

» **Be proactive.** Anticipate a problem before it happens.

» **Have a goal** and plan in mind, but go with the flow.

» **Refuse to give in** to negative beliefs (not smart enough, not good enough, powerless, or don't know enough).

» **"You are braver than you believe, stronger than you seem, and smarter than you think."**
—A.A. Milne

» **Focus on surviving** and maintaining your health. This will keep you from dwelling on anything else.

» **NEVER** give up!

NATURE CAN BE CRUEL AND UNFORGIVING, BUT WHEN A PERSON FACES IT HEAD-ON, HE OR SHE WILL SURVIVE.

MASK YOUR SCENT

Most dinosaurs have a great sense of smell, just like modern-day birds. However, there are a few things you can do to mask your scent so the dinosaurs won't even know you're there.

» **Wash your clothes** with baking soda. Never use detergent.

» **Dry your clothes** on a clothesline.

» **Take a shower.** Use unscented soaps and shampoos.

» Use vanilla-flavored chewing gum or chlorophyll tablets to **mask your breath.**

» Break a branch with leaves off of a tree or grab a handful of grass from the area and rub it all over yourself.

» **Stand downwind** of any dinosaur. If you stand upwind, it will catch your scent.

NOTE: Make sure you aren't grabbing a handful of poisonous plant, such as poison ivy, poison sumac, or poison oak.

Some people think that covering yourself in dinosaur poop or pee will mask your scent. It won't work! Either you're marking yourself with the scent of a plant-eater and will attract every meat-eater in the area, or you're marking yourself as a meat-eater, which could invite other meat-eaters to challenge you for the territory. Just step away from the dino poop!

USE CAMOUFLAGE

If you've masked your scent, but the dinosaurs are still coming after you, try camouflage. Some dinosaurs didn't have great vision, but others could see like hawks. Camouflage will help you blend into your surroundings. Here are some ways to blend in:

» Use the color patterns and textures in your area.

» Put small tree branches, vines, and grasses on your body to hide in plain sight.

» Cover all of your exposed skin areas with charcoal or mud. Be sure to use an irregular pattern.

» **Stay in the shadows.**

» Keep as much vegetation between you and the dinosaur as possible.

» Keep your movements slow or don't move at all. Fast movement attracts attention.

» Try to avoid making any loud noises. Use background noise, like strong wind or rain, to hide your movements.

How to Create a Dinosaur Trip Wire

Let's face it. The most dangerous dinosaurs to your survival will be the meat-eaters. Set a trip wire trap for them. Here's how.

What You'll Need:

- Fishing line, wire, or rope
- Nails
- Duct tape
- Hammer

1. Find a path that goes between two trees.

2. Wrap your rope, wire, or fishing line around one tree about 12 in. (30.5 cm) from the ground. Tie it off with a bowline loop knot.

3. String it across the path and tie the other end around the second tree the same way.

4. Wrap duct tape around the loops to keep them from coming undone.

5. Wait for your dinosaur to appear.

This is one of the most used loop knots. It's simple and secure. Use it to secure a rope to a tree.

BOWLINE LOOP KNOT

MY SURVIVAL LIST

WHAT WILL YOU HAVE READY WHEN THE DINOSAURS INVADE YOUR NEIGHBORHOOD? MAKE A LIST OF WHAT YOU'LL NEED TO DO, FIND, OR BRING TO KEEP YOU AND YOUR FAMILY SAFE.

DINOSAUR
SURVIVAL QUIZ

1. If an Eoraptor is in your house, you should . . .
A. Cower in fear.
B. Run at it with a chair.
C. Be very, very quiet and let it move on.

2. A Carnotaurus is a very friendly dinosaur.
A. It's like a house pet.
B. It's not so scary.
C. It is one of the Top 10 Most Deadly Dinosaurs.

3. You are alone in the woods and hear rustling in the bushes. You . . .
A. Ask, Why am I in the woods?
B. Turn and run.
C. Stand very still. The dinosaur should move past you.

4. Stegosaurus is a meat-eating dinosaur.
A. Okay, if you say so.
B. Yeah, that sounds right.
C. Uh, no! It eats plants.

5. What do you do if you see a Compsognathus hunting?
A. Go up to it and hand it some birdseed.
B. Run really fast the other way.
C. Freeze and don't make a sound.

6. Covering yourself with dinosaur poop will help you blend in with the other dinosaurs.
A. Ew! But okay.
B. Uh, no thanks!
C. I'd rather take a baking soda bath.

7. It is best to stand upwind of an animal to hide your scent.
A. Um . . . I know this one.
B. Yes, that's right.
C. No, downwind is better.

8. Which dinosaur is thought to be the most intelligent?
A. Diplodocus
B. Allosaurus
C. Troodon

WATCH OUT!

9. **Which of the following dinosaurs is the most dangerous?**
A. Ankylosaurus
B. A pack of Velociraptors
C. Tyrannosaurus rex

10. **A family member or friend is hurt in a dinosaur attack. What do you do?**
A. Scream like a little girl.
B. Run away. You don't want to get hurt, too.
C. Get them to a safe place and bandage their wound. After all, you took that first aid course.

11. **An invasive species are . . .**
A. Zombies?
B. Never around when you need one.
C. Animals that aren't normally found in a certain area

12. **What is the best way to prepare yourself for the dinosaur invasion?**
A. Run away
B. Put a survival bag together?
C. Read this book!

IF YOU ANSWERED MOSTLY A'S:

You really need to read this book. You're not ready for the dinosaur invasion and may become extinct.

IF YOU ANSWERED MOSTLY B'S:

You're getting there. You know more than most people about dinosaurs, but you need to know more to survive. Go back and review the information a few more times.

IF YOU ANSWERED MOSTLY C'S:

You are a dinosaur whiz and are ready for the invasion. Make sure you have your list and map ready to go before the dinosaurs get to your neighborhood.

GLOSSARY

adaptation — a change in an organism over time that better enables it to survive.

crampons — a set of steel spikes that fit on the bottom of a climbing boot to give better grip on icy slopes or snow.

frequency — the number of sound waves that pass a fixed point each second

latrine — a bathroom or toilet

omnivore — a being that feeds on both animals and plants

paleontologist — a scientist who deals with the life of the past, especially from fossil remains

scavenger - an organism that usually feeds on dead or decaying matter

theropods — a carnivorous dinosaur group whose member walked on two legs and range from small and delicate to very large

warm-blooded - able to keep a constant body temperature that is mostly independent of the surrounding environment.